Gravity

Gravity

POEMS BY

JOHN MINCZESKI

Texas Tech University Press

Jacket and Book Design by Joanna Hill.
Jacket art by Thomas C. Minczeski

Manufactured in the United States of America

Library of Congress Cataloging-in-Publication Data

Minczeski, John.
      Gravity : poems / by John Minczeski.
         p. cm.
      ISBN 0–89672–267–8 (alk. paper). — ISBN 0–89672–268–6 (pbk. :
alk. paper)
      I. Title.
PS3563.I4635G73 1991
811'.54—dc20   91–18736
                                                                            CIP

91 92 93 94 95 96 97 98 99 / 9 8 7 6 5 4 3 2 1

Texas Tech University Press
Lubbock, Texas 79409–1037 USA

iv

To my daughter, Jessica

Acknowledgments

Grateful acknowledgment is made to the following journals, in which some of these poems, some in earlier versions, first appeared:

Abraxas: "Asparagus," "Phelps Municipal Dump"
ACM: "A Drunk at the Tennis Court," "Native Tongue"
Farmer's Market: "Water Striders"
Free Lunch: "Thaw"
Menomonie Review: "Eve"
Mr. Cogito: "Columbines"
Poet & Critic: "Elvis Impersonator at the World's
    Largest Office Party: La Crosse, Wisconsin," "First
    Grader"
Northeast: "A Poet in the Schools: Brainerd, Minnesota"
Pendragon: "Woman at the Cool Bar: Elgin, North
    Dakota, 1949"

"Watched Clocks" appeared originally in *Journey Notes,*
Hazelden and Harper and Row. "Asphalt" appeared
originally in *Concert at Chopin's House: A Collection of Polish
American Writing,* New Rivers Press.

I would like to acknowledge the assistance of the Bush
Foundation and the National Endowment for the Arts for
fellowships that allowed me time to write some of these
poems, the Loft and the McKnight Foundation for a writing
grant, and the Ragdale Foundation for generous use of its
facilities.

Contents

I

Icarus

Other instructors waited by the flight shack
when they soloed students:
three take-offs, three landings, six Hail Marys.
But my father stood in the middle of the airfield
keeping me glued with his eyes to the traffic pattern,
the way I used to guide my model airplane,
its mosquito-drone engine at the end of a control line.

And I remembered, too, *him* taking off,
the plane shrinking into a dot,
and shaved invisible with a blink.

Now I was sixteen. He stood next to the taxiway,
small as a pea, having ridden along
on a few practice landings—one for my mother,
watching from the car and crying,
one for him, one for me—then told the tower
he was turning this bird loose and got out of the plane.
Bird—it sounded so final, what I had wanted.

Book Report

The fifth grader stands in front of the blackboard
reading what he copied from the blurb.
A couple of sentences and his chore is done.
The teacher could have just marked another *F*
next to his name, and said "nice try, Jeff,"
but she decides it is time
to save him. Does his report
mention a specific character, she asks, an event,
a single location?
He stands tapping his foot,
like a guitarist slouching into his instrument
as the air grows loose and granular
with a wheezing like an air conditioner except
it is winter and the snow is starting.
Try again,
read the book this time, she says from her desk
as though behind a stack of junked tires,
and he shuffles to his seat
having successfully stuck himself in the future
and waited for the moment to catch up.
He can start tapping even faster now,
like running a film fast forward
to summer, his bicycle, the beach.
The snow picks up, cloudy swirls
trail off eaves and make the wind
visible. School will be called tomorrow
but he is there already,

shoveling, sledding.
He jams his report deep in his desk; the papers
all nest together.
Come June they'll molt
in a black plastic bag. Then
is practically today—
all the freedom he'll ever need
lies the other side of that final bell.

A Poet in the Schools: Brainerd, Minnesota

Lost from exhaustion after teaching all day,
I cranked up Mozart and closed my eyes
into the D minor piano concerto.
A woman stood before me then
and seemed to ask why her arms were so empty.
Her white dress—it was like nothing,
or a ghost, arms out like Eurydice
the moment before she slid back down,
the reflected light beginning to strike her face,
her sandals barely scraping rock. . .
A sob broke free from the muck
at the bottom of sleep and bobbed up
to a world where, as a fourth grader wrote,
they tear the wings off angels.
All week they've kept their heads bowed
as if chained to their desks,
and in the last row between light and the blackboard,
my down-filled coat slumped. They called it *Hermie*,
first for "Herman," and then for the apostle of quickness
who can be in two places at once.
The blue fabric worn shiny—almost black.
"How's Hermie," they'd call when I entered
with sacks full of books and poems.
I'd give the thumbs-up and plop him at an empty desk.
He can sleep anywhere, I told them, desperate
for a little joy.

Mid-September

for Davida Kilgore

In the petalled shade of the still-green chokecherry,
and over the red plump sedum, the air almost like moss on
    brick,
the day closes. What could be more cruel
than the deep blue of evening
which keeps us on the fine edge of sanity—
an airplane to Paris where it's too soon morning?
They've already fired the bakery ovens there
as beeline streets get tricked into light.

How can one say *the light deepens,* except that, here,
the harvest moon is like a false dawn
and the clear night *almost* starless.
Since you left, the nights keep growing
into faint northern lights
we can just make out from the city.

As the world tilts on its axis,
as you move against its spin, the bees sleep unaware
of the displacement—there is work tomorrow,
the sedum blossoming into a dance, a song,
until it powers them and they take off.

Night Hawks

The old Aeronca Champ slow-rolled
like a sack of potatoes, buffeting
until it seemed the plexiglass would pop,
the stall warning screaming bloody murder—
when I tried a stunt named after Max Immelmann,
the whole control panel flared orange,
flashed and sizzled until I rolled out.
The sparks weren't close enough to the fuel line
for me to die then—
nineteen-years-old and a fear and love of death.
I dreamed the bomb came again and again
and woke sitting in bed
full of sweat and the end of the world.

I spent more than I made
flying the Aeronca that year,
wheel-landings and split-Ss,
rode motorcycles full out until the oil seals blew,
and figured I would live somehow,
maybe to fall as a night hawk does,
a shriek as it pulls out of its dive,
g-forces pressing down
its wings pulling up with a whoosh
between the close-packed roof overhangs
and the slow flapping in sluggish air
to get back above the world, squawking
to fall again,

wings against my back,
and with the terrible, wonderful speed
the fall gives, *up*
at the final moment.

The Snake

Slid off the foot-bridge quickly
and swam toward new invisibility
into the underbrush on the bank,
triangle head and brown diamond shapes.
You said it wasn't poisonous and avoided panic.
Later, in the encyclopedia, there it was,
brown on brown, beside the Eastern Diamond Back.
"A beauty," I said
as we leaned over the rail; and it was,
as death always is as it moves away.

The Devil's Hand

I saw him once, as I walked past an alley woodpile.
I was six, and there he was,
his hand, rather,
that looked like the black paw of a dog
thrashing up from the cast-off lumber,
and as if gathering something back to himself,
crashing down again.
My friends hadn't seen, though they walked beside me;
they said yes, it had to be the devil,
and so near.
All evening, in the fading light
we told the neighbor girls,
who had seen him also
in laundry chutes, or disappearing
behind shrubbery. We had become,
without meaning to, a secret group,
all six or seven of us, even the one
who saw him in the doorway of her bedroom
and was so scared
she jumped out of her skin
and stayed on the wall, next to the ceiling.
And nothing she saw was a sin,
since she was hardly there
to feel what happened.

Watched Clocks

for Richard Solly

First it was a small pain
then it was bigger than the world
and made itself at home in the hospital
where my friend stared at the clock,
pain emptying him
until the thinner he became
the greater the pain by proportion.
He looked from the clock, to the window,
to me, to the window, to the clock.
He closed his eyes
and pain opened them with a jerk.
He thought it would take the Demerol
ten minutes to kick in, then ten more.
I wet the cloth on his forehead
as the Demerol worked slower than the minutes.
I tried to make the room light
but it didn't help.
Maybe what saved his life
was he didn't eat. The nurse said
she'd leave the tray
in case he changed his mind.
I wiped a towel around his face
rasping on whisker stubble, mopping up sweat.
Now he says "Pain! Go Away!"
but he can't say it strong enough

for pain to hear.
I tell him they'll have to pull
the ice-houses off the lakes tomorrow.
He looks at me, *tomorrow,*
and looks at the clock;
pain lakes, pain thaw. His eyes
shift to the wall, the clock, my face,
the window with afternoon shadows
growing down from the blue,
then back to me.
You're going to write this down,
aren't you, pain says
from deep in his eyes. I shake my head.
My friend seems to relax a second
when pain simply reaches down
and twists so hard
he straightens like a board.
Everything's so easy
pain gets everything it wants now.

Trout Fishing with My Brother

for Matthew Minczeski

My brother stands on the bank watching trout
nose into the current like torpedoes.
He waves off a mosquito from his ear,
he brushes his face, his nose
and he is always my brother,
the small awkwardnesses I see in myself,
mute stumblings on mud-slick,
suddenly leaning against a tree.
He makes his way downstream as a bear might
before the four-footed lunge,
the squirming fish in a claw. The trout
bump into my spoon to sniff and sidle away;
monofilament hangs from overhead branches:
bobbers, bare trout-hooks, sinkers.
My brother says I look like Uncle Ray
white bearded, white haired, casting
from the bridge. But all I catch
is snag after snag;
a moment of air between me and water,
a breath.

Grandfather Janosz and
the Polish Graves of New Prague

With neon from the bar lighting the snow
that swirls past my knees, it looks like
I'm walking through the ground
halfway among the dead taking it easy
zgoda, zgoda, above the earth and below.

Seven languages he racked up
knocking from country to country.
Four of them he spoke well
and they all boiled down to Polish.

That spring when Ned brought a box of dirt
back from Poland, we baked the living crap
out of it first, then sprinkled it,
grey powder, over the graves.

An old lady grabbed my hand to kiss.
Her Stanley, she said, was home now, at peace,
repeating the Polish *zgoda,* peace, peace.
All that weeping, but it was only Poland.

First Grader

When the Indian kid says
he would jump off a bridge and drown himself
to make someone like him, his classmates
circle their ears with their fingers
to make the "screwy" sign.

I think I know where he has in mind—a bridge
where the river empties into Lake Bemidji
and keeps it clear of ice. He would last fifteen seconds
in the December water before his clothes and the current
dragged him out under the ice.

He doesn't have to jump, I tell him, for me to like him.
He stares at an eraser he turns over in his hands
as if he can squeeze into himself
its power to smudge out mistakes.
I wouldn't like him, he says, if he got mad.

I'm too much of a stranger, up from the cities
for a few days only, a few words on the board
that disappear into chalk dust and air,
as he would disappear under the lake.

He sinks
into his eraser, his heart on the ground,

as a Sioux friend would say,
almost at one with the horizon

and his chair, like all the others,
is close to the ground, too,
so he won't have far to go
when he falls or jumps.

Icing Up

A Cessna 182 in sloppy snow,
ice scabbing the wings and prop—
the controls in my father's hands
turned mushy and shook, the ice-altered
shape of the wing meant the nose
would pitch down soon,
a block of ice in a patch of ice.

Three-quarters of a mile up, full throttle,
the prop screwed into high rpm, the clear ice
made our wing little more than a shovel
slipping under the radar of traffic control.
I could not imagine the hole we would make,
or a farmer telling the sheriff's deputy
how the engine revved and snarled,
and how it sounded like nothing
as when a mower conks out in thick grass.
What could I tell my father,
who had flown the wounded
back from Karachi and Kabul in the war,
to check the snap into stall and spin?
He was near fifty, I was nineteen; we would never
be so close again, nearly melted together
into steel tubing, instruments, rich earth.

We broke into the clear then
and from the ground must have looked beautiful

trailing sparkles of death as though fresh
from the birth canal, more angel than airplane,
going full bore. Ice cracked off in chunks,
the air awakened, buoyant—so much for luck.

My father hitched a ride home in a Twin Beech,
de-icing boots on the wings;
I flew on to Austin, a trip too routine to remember,
and we breathed into separate lives
further and further apart from each other
and that precise moment
a crack of a second *before* it was too late,
when the blue surfaced and ran, amazed,
clear around the world.

II

Ice Fishermen

Huddling against the wind in great parkas,
in thick boots and snow pants and enormous mittens,
their faces, under their hoods, red and hard
as the swollen faces of Chicago traffic cops,

they've augured through the lake's navel
and set up buzzers and bells on the ends of their rods
so when a fish strikes
they'll pull it through to this world.

Maybe one hacks out a bigger hole
before he can drag out his northern,
conk it on the head, pack it in snow
as the others stamp their feet
and exhale solemn clouds of breath.

It is too cold for words.
Every afternoon—for as long as the ice
can support them—they stand in a circle,
three of them, waiting for fish,
while the dark
slowly rises through the ice holes
and hardens.

Hauntings

He used to think he knew his house so well
he could go through it
as a ship does, without lights,

but when the lady next door died
he was afraid she'd drop by his house
and when he bent for a beer
from the small fridge in the spare bedroom
she'd be sitting on the futon,
patient and slightly confused.

But it was his cat
at the bottom of the stairs
who screeched when he stepped on it
and sank its claws in his ankle,
not any spirit. It tore away
for the middle of the room
where it could eye him, who couldn't see.

Sometimes, on the sultriest nights,
thinking he hears women's voices
over the noise of the fan,

he turns on the lights, checks the house,
lets the cats in from the porch.

As they shift to lick themselves on the warm TV,
pressing the channel-buttons all night,
blue electron snow sifts and glows.

Eve

While he sleeps, light crawls
toward darkness on its hands and knees
a rib held between its teeth,
and Eve springs full-bodied into the sanctuary.

They will soon know love,
will cry out and draw back.
But now they sleep—
the green buds
peel back like centuries.

One by one she lives through them
until it is Chicago
and she works behind the glass
at a self-service gas station.
It is 1982: of two children
one has turned out bad.

Opening her eyes,
she looks into the other, astonished face,
his lips moving soundlessly.
Already her dream is slipping
from one darkness into another,

as his fingers, she can feel them now,
begin to open the doors of her body.

The Fight

It was like a ballet
that broke out of nowhere
at 3 a.m., a Country Kitchen
in Alexandria, Minnesota,
as chairs scooched back and tipped over.

There were no words
for what it meant:
language had broken down
into grunts and thuds;

life had given them fists,
hammy cheeks, coffee
and half a donut lying on a table
next to the waitress tray.
The night manager
simply stepped to the phone and dialed.

You would have thought they loved each other,
the way their faces looked,
they could have been related.
Everything so quiet,
even the police car
pulled up with its siren off

after the two guys got into cars
and drove away. Everyone knew

who it was and where they'd gone
to sleep it off, and they told the cops,
"they was waltzing."

Woman at the Cool Bar:
Elgin, North Dakota, 1949

from a photograph by Frank Agar

I thought it was Spain at first
because I didn't know people smiled in North Dakota.
The woman's polka-dotted dress, her kerchief
are elements of gravity, as is a half glass of beer,
but her face, it is the moon.

She smiles, her friends are smiling,
and Frank Agar, who is much younger,
is taking the picture: like a dream
he walked into the bar,
ordered a beer, set up his tripod.
Are you from Fargo, she asked.

It is summer, the bar clock reads five of three.
I am two-years-old and have just tried
to climb into the barnyard at my great-uncle's farm.
Anything large with four legs is a horse.
I am crying, more angry than hurt,
as my brother drags me back from the fence.

These people are not crying, their teeth
are large and well-spaced, and they don't care
if we ever make it to the moon.

Elvis Impersonator at the World's Largest Office Party: La Crosse, Wisconsin

I never saw Elvis, and now there are so many—
like Santas warming themselves at firepots,
white beards and false stomachs.
At least this one has real hair and jowls,
high collar and black fringes—
Elvis circa 1969, *The Vegas Years*—
there's that pouty turn to his lips as he says
how much Elvis meant to him growing up,
Canton, Ohio, 1963.

It's that part of the evening
when the show turns personal.
Because we love Elvis, we might,
if we give it half a chance, love each other.
Why not ask someone to dance, or at least sing along.
He steps back for the downbeat, the two
backup singers go *Ooh Wah Wah,*
but the evening has collapsed into singles,
wine coolers in plastic cups,
sweeping the horizons like radar dishes.

Out in the parking lot where I go
to be swallowed by night,
a little of the bass guitar survives.
It thuds right through me and keeps going.

Wood Fires

Smoke from wood fires drifts through the village
and walking around I get whiffs
of birch and poppel and slow-going oak
becoming ash inside the furnaces
which must be tended carefully, fed and emptied,

for we are married to winter, as they were in another village
in the mountains, their stoves burning
prunings of grape vines and olive trees.
Parsimonious about heat, they used it
only for cooking, or baths,
since they had to buy the wood
from men who carried it bundled on their backs,
more twisted than the trees the branches came from.

So we sat in the kitchen where heat's alchemy
turned water and bone into soup, flour into noodles;
a rooster, trussed, breathed in the corner
by a basket of onions and garlic braids.

One whiff of wood smoke still slams me
against those times, fresh from a dream
where I kissed a local girl
and held her, looking at neighboring mountains.
It turned to smoke in me, that kiss,
invisible, or barely blue.

Monkey Trees

In the Po Valley, the trees cluttering the fields
had been pruned severely over the years—
skinny branches springing from wooly trunks
like porcupine quills—there was no other word
than what my daughter gave them, *Monkey Trees,*
from the train. Delighted with her power to name,
she kept pointing and laughing
until I was afraid an Italian would take offense,
or think us stupid.
But anger was an old woman in black
saying loudly from the aisle, in Italian,
three people taking a whole compartment
while others have to stand, how shameful,
looking straight at me, our bags scattered
where we dropped them, exhausted, relieved
for second-class seats. Her hollow eye sockets
reminded me of the woman in my night terrors,
the feverish-greasy other side of religion,
Medusa shrieking, her snakes hidden.
As monkey trees flashed by the windows,
I heaved and wedged the luggage overhead,
and thinking to show
she frightened me no longer, closed my eyes.
It was dark when I awoke,
a Milan youth choir had burst into song
as we slowed into the Rome terminus,

and I felt the mental post cards arrive
that I had sent myself fifteen years before.
I didn't know if the hag
had gotten off by then, but the singing,
the first balmy night of spring,
all these smiling people—it was enough
to drown anyone in joy.

Asparagus

A glass of water with spears of asparagus
Orlando found walking on the mountain—
"Look," he says, "remember?"
We had talked an hour in the other room
about Carlo and Ilych, but mostly Margherita,
dead these six months.
Now we sit in the kitchen—
a bedroom fifteen years before
when I went with him and his grown son
to hunt asparagus.

In her kitchen, Margherita ruled
with wands of asparagus,
telling stories of unfaithful wives
whose husbands set them on top of stoves—
she made a sizzling sound through her teeth
and waved her hand upward like smoke.
When my girlfriend wrote
that everything was over between us,
Margherita said, "When the Pope dies, find another."
Others in the kitchen took up the cry,
"When the pope dies, get another."

Now Orlando eats from the bowl he serves from.
Now *his* kitchen where skinny asparagus
stick out of a glass next to the sink.

Wild ones, a flavor of the mountains.
"My friend, dear John," he says,
"I am like the son here,
now that the house has gone to Bruna.
If you wait another fifteen years to come back
I won't be here."

He would like to set up a tent
next to the tenements of death—
"*Caro* John," he says, "it doesn't matter anymore
who's American or Communist;
once the missiles start flying,
it's the end of all of us—
bad enough living under the fascists."

And the asparagus,
whose roots spread down to former civilizations
are a gift from the dead to the living,
part of the Easter feast, and a sign:
for one more year, earth has pulled through.
Spear grass, sparrow grass, I felt its pull
fifteen years ago with Orlando and Giorgio
on the grassy slope of Monteluco.

Monteluco

What good is a mountain unless
you can climb it, especially one full
of roots and shrub for hand and footholds?
And what good is climbing
unless you look down from a hundred feet up,
feel the cheap gravel give beneath you,
and grab on to something as if
its green purpose was put there
to trust your small life to? What good is any place
unless you've left a portion of your shadow behind,
a little piece of death—
                       what good is death
without smaller deaths strewn
in places like Monteluco, "Holy Mountain" to the Romans,
a clump of holm oaks pursuing their destiny
among red spikes of sumac,
where I heard goat bells but saw no goats,
where I stood
halfway between the ground and the great blue sky.

All that time, all those clanking bells
saying *here I am*, and no easy way down.
So I climbed, scratched and bruised,
from sapling to rock and weedclump until the sun
ready to be swallowed by the purpled sea,

shone on a covered watercourse
and I walked its slabs alongside the mountain,
a tiny road from the middle ages that led
to the goatpath that led to a larger road,
into the world, that led here.

Columbines

Columbines are blooming right now,
between the honeysuckle and bleeding heart,
tucked out of sight, quietly
like their cousins in Jelenie Gora,

so barely blue they could be used
for prototypes of a future that shoots ahead
and backward at the same time. Grackles,
in washboard voices no one understands,
give orders from the garage I'll tear down soon.
I'm already nostalgic for its swayback roof
and useless sentry boxes beside the broken door.

There are no chickens here and the sky is clouding over.
This is not a country where flowers are handed down
generation after generation; I don't know Polish,
and I'm losing an argument among these red flowers
that will never resemble blood, and blue ones
so pale they have given up claims to royalty forever.

Phelps Municipal Dump

A day between rains
and the municipal dump is closed.
We haul garbage on foot
up past the curve of blacktop,
past white fridges and stoves

to a pit where a man
tending small clots of fire
motions broadly—as pines
steeple over rusty
caterpillar tractors—

Toss it anywhere!
Our cardboard box tumbles
into the center of the continent
beneath the jowls of Lake Superior.
On the right side of the road

rosy clusters of smoke
turn into raspberries—tunnels
leading into sunset's cul-de-sac.
Ah, purgatory,
we're eating our way home.

for ACH

A Drunk at the Tennis Court

My brother and I went to Leeper Park
to bat a tennis ball over the net,
but spent most of our time searching
under the skirts of bushes for the grey ball.
Early June,
and out of school for the next three months—

something made us turn and look
at a guy wearing a winter coat,
leaning against a light standard
to heave up something black:
we were too far to hear the coughing and retching,
but I thought he might be having a heart attack.
When my brother turned to me,
I gave my head a small shake,
we were nine and twelve, what did we know?

We went on with our game,
trying not to look at the street
where the man had lain down
in the shade of oak and maple

to die a little more in peace.
A patrol car, Studebaker Lark, eased to the curb,
and two cops pulled on gloves
before they lifted him into the back seat.

No longer interested in the game,
one of us bashed the ball
into a clump of spirea where we left it,
and avoiding where the guy had been,
crossed the Michigan Street bridge
and four more blocks, half-aware
and not daring to admit it,
that all we had was each other.

Native Tongue

Another year I have not settled in New York
or walked the park in grey tweeds:
at 10:30 my window and the street light, sweaty with sleet,
stand against the mutual admiration of ice and night.

I waited for the word to become light and dwell among us
like an efficient carburetor; I asked for chocolate
and received vanilla. It wasn't for me
to wear the cast-off robes of angels,

like my friend, P., who could tell you
of a cafe in Rome where the future is being written
or hold an empty glass and say our destiny is inside,
but no one's heard from him

since he went off to live in the streets.
It's easy to imagine the St. Joe River,
black against snow, or plastic seats
in the Greyhound Station, since I was also born mad,

and stuff my hands in the pockets of my overcoat
so I look hump-backed, my grandfather's accent rasping
against the back of my throat like a lamp
all night calling me back to my native tongue.

The End of the World

Grand Forks might not
be the end of the world,
but you can see it from there.
                    Mark Vinz

North of Grand Forks where missile silos stretch
almost to Canada in chain link fences,
the end of the world waits quietly underground.
A few houses, lit up in the pre-dawn,
ride the gently rolling prairie
where a hundred years ago farmers hauled wheat by ox-cart
to the Fargo Market.

The winter it hit eighty-five below
the guy driving me to work said,
fifteen miles this side of nowhere,
how about I drop you off here,
and I couldn't tell if he was trying to be funny.
I said I'd try to freeze standing up
with my arm raised so the rescue party
would know where to start digging.

The wind wove white braids on the road
as it kept pushing us toward the ditch
drifted brown and grey with topsoil and snow.
That night, behind the motel,
a mobile home filled with electricity;

a rusted-out Ford Falcon rested on blocks;
a few trees lined the river—beyond them
I could see nothing.

Thaw

It is mire and muck down to the frost line,
all melt through the flooded fields;
an intermittent sky, encroaching woods
as I drive; every dip in the road's another culvert
through which the spring thaw shoots mud and sky
just this side of ice
swollen out of the muscles of snow
as the run-off grinds through sandstone,
more diamond than water.

At Pine City the river deserves its name
Snake, except it roars instead of rattles
as it twists and rolls like fire
drawing a million sirens towards its smoke
and calls a two-year-old who waits
until his mother's back is turned.
Three weeks later the river's tame again.
The parents stand outside their cabin
saying to reporters *he's gone back,*
he's just gone back. The newsmen
pause, the camera augurs in.

The men in hip boots have given up dragging
and gone to hand-tied flies. How deaf I am, driving past
that moment the river wailed,

stampede bulging in the middle, tearing out
trees and banks, gnawing itself and craving
anything this once besides itself,
anybody's child.

III

Dirigible

It was 1932, I think, San Diego,
the newsreel showed two men falling to their deaths,
sailors who had been holding down the *Akron.*
When it bucked in the wind, the other sailors
let the mooring lines go, and in a snap
the ground fell away leaving three men dangling.
The first who couldn't hold on any more
tucked his arms and legs into himself
like a diver before the final spring into water,
his eyes closed, and in the rush of air
seemed to leave his body. The second one
clawed desperately, as if climbing a ladder,
to slow those long, last seconds,
twisting around, mid-way, to climb
facing the other direction,
but the plume of dust when he hit
joined the other one, fanning out
over the heads of crew and spectators
as the third sailor tied the loose end of the line
to his waist and seemed to stand calmly
in the middle of the air,
under the billowy keel of the enormous cocoon
breaking away from the earth
and was hauled up
to the only safety left.

My Father's Kitchen

I don't know when he started hating Blacks or why,
though we argued hours in his kitchen,
fake brick pasted to one wall like grief.

In '65, when riots started to blister
and he drove close enough to get spotted,
I don't know if any rocks hit the car,
just that he threw it into reverse
and hauled ass back to this side of the river.

And I didn't know my flesh would take on his age and
    wrinkles,
as we sat facing each other, his bitterness become mine
until neither my mother nor my wife could pry us apart
from our friable mass of English—
that I would match him mask for mask
as we glared in those black vinyl chairs.
Dirty Commie, he hissed.
I raised my beer and smiled in his face.

How many generations back in Poland,
a farmer's hovel with dirt floor
and dirtier logic, did they also think
there could be a winner? There was only mirror

and reflection. The dark
rose from the bottom of the river.
We were the last ones awake, we had forgotten
the others, could have gone on sitting there
for a hundred years without moving,
without any sign of surrender.

No Easy Way

The bat stuck between the screen and window
doesn't melt into skeleton and Dracula dust
at day break, it tries to hang
from the sash edge so it can sleep,
but loses its grip, shudders then falls.
By noon its muscles seem to spasm
as it climbs the screen, its body
outlined against the thin membrane wing
like a man climbing a chain-link fence.
I raise the screen a little,
but the bat doesn't fall far enough to know
it can let itself out. It scrapes glass,
making a blackboard sound,
wanting inside the house. But I have decided
the world outside is better—
a god who wants to see a little despair
once the bat lies at the bottom of the sill,
and the disbelief, the double-take
when it musters itself
to push up on long fingers and tail,
to edge over the aluminum lip
of the combination window
and take flight toward the trees
in the middle of the day.
So much for free will.
Partly I wanted it to say *no,*

and climb up the screen
over the gap to begin again,
as if the way out
can be the same as the way in,
as Theseus knew, wanted it to say
enough tricks, you bastard, even when
either way, it enters the same world.

Water Striders

I slip on the bank, grab a branch
to steady myself and stomp the mud near shore.
Water striders skate with their Jesus-feet,
scribbling something
to the fish beneath
or to some angel looking on,
but it's quickly erased in the current.
Each a St. Christopher
bearing a gene-pool on its back, feeding and mating,
tuned to the minute electrical pulses
of water, they look forward
to the strider
who will build the temple of water
and serve enemies up on little platters;
who will say blessed are the meek,
they will shine golden like the sun,
and shall comfort themselves,
the bad trout have been taken up.
Eat therefore the river lice,
the tiny shrimp, drink this water,
it is for you,
it is just for you.

Asphalt

At St. Stan's, back in seventh grade,
a black girl was sweet on my friend, Dave.
Her name was Diane, and when she passed the playground
on her way to Linden School after lunch,
along with two friends who were shy
in this suddenly white world,
Dave would hide behind a clump of boys
trying to act as if chain reactions weren't happening,
desperately looking for some horizon to gaze beyond.
If she found him, she had him walk her
part way to her school, her two friends hurrying ahead;
or she'd take a swipe at him with her pocketbook.
Sometimes she'd sing out, "Oh boys, have you seen Dave?"

When I, maybe out of jealousy
at what could have been love,
and maybe to honor it, pointed him out
in the alcove that led to the boiler room,
he shoved me into a wall—
part of me smiled, sweaty
with seventh grade. Eighth grade
she didn't come around any more—
a rumor goes she had a kid and got on welfare.
After graduation I never saw Dave again, either,
but I find myself thinking about the kid,

twenty-five or -six now, standing beside a white Chevy
as kids shoot baskets behind the school.
It must be spring—there's a smell to the air
that makes everything stand still,
except for the thunk of basketball against backboard,
a rattle from the bone-bare hoop, and he goes on waiting,
so caught in the moment all else disappears—
Diane, Dave, all that might have been, all that was.

My Brother Shoots My Daughter's Portrait: Oakland, California, 1986

One eye to the viewfinder, he works the lens
so the world behind it is as clear
as the world his other eye, screwed shut, would see.
My daughter, surrounded by silvered umbrellas,
sits on a wicker clothes hamper.
Look up, he says, *think of something funny,*
beautiful, beautiful—
she leans into the camera,
raising a shoulder, smiling, pouting,
shaking her hair.
In her silence, her half-grin could say anything.
Snapping a close-up lens on the Nikon,
he jokes about capturing her soul,
winks, wiggles his hips, trying to be cool,
to drop the tangled syntax of *adult*
and *sixteen-year-old*, while I look on from another world
silently and nervously, separate from the performance.
When he straightens up and she relaxes her back,
the fireplace behind the backdrop
is once again a fireplace.
Only the film's emulsion,
like a specimen on a lab slide,
shows what was sliced neatly out,
with no wound or scar, no sense of anything missing.

Two Bugs

Green Beetle on Warren Wilson Mountain

As if covered in satin
and ready to step out
into the formal evening—
green legs, green shell, clean and shiny
with black opal segments underneath.
We want you to fly, we want to see
a flash of green across the sun,
but when we pick you up on a stick
to tease your wings open,
there is only a slow orchestration of legs,
green sheathed, green world, green time.
We turn you over and praise you—
sharp antennae, bow of back,
scarab shivering in the pre-dusk
after a meal of aphids, slug, poison ivy,
nine-tenths of the god inhabiting the universe.
And we let you live, my teacher and I,
something like good thieves, hoping
for a kind word once you've made it home
on this mountain that rolls down,
that rolls down to the river below.

Monarch

Among the purple spikes of liatris,
black veined wings fold together—
stained glass, weathervane.
Once I wandered into a fury of migration—
they fluttered around me
as if to bring me out of gravity
with an orange halo; as if saying
believe, you can walk on air.
Long after they must have known
I would not rise,
they circled in that silence,
that desire.

Pulling Vines

After the roses stopped flowering, the canes,
thin and barbed, spread through the tomato vines
like assassins' whips; so when I bent to pluck
a ripe tomato, drops of blood were left in its place.

It should have brought a sweetening
as in faery tales—the hardest labor, the greatest reward.
But they were so dryly acidic,
the tomatoes the slugs didn't get first we left in the window
until dark and pulpy and I lobbed them
toward the compost heap.

The day after harvest moon I dragged the vines,
still heavy with fruit, down the driveway
like shriven sins, not waiting for the first real frost
to mull them. Mosquitoes had their way with me;
the bees hovered, sniffing.

Who was it said Rilke pricked himself on a rose thorn
and died three days later? I left the canes on the concrete
where over winter they'll turn black
as figs. Now I weed the garden.
This is not the end of the sensual life, it is just
September, half-way through, and I must make room for
    more.

Gravity

1. Portrait with Hands

Driving to McGregor, my fingers on the wheel
seem longer than usual—filaments almost
stretching into the night, probing
and guiding me through
as I swerve right to avoid a smashed cat
with a flick of the wrist
like a wing banking and leveling off.

Outside the video store yesterday
when a couple of four-year-olds on scooters yelled
Hi Grandpa! and laughed, I thought
to let my anger out, but climbed
into my grandfather's skin
to laugh with them. And yesterday
my wife and I laughed after making love
the almost wheezing way we had propelled ourselves
toward light, as if wading through elephant grass
and suddenly coming upon ocean.

I look at my hands now
and they are just hands:
veiny road maps, blood rushing heartward;
part of me knows the way home.

2. *Ways of Bringing It In*

You can bring a plane in like a dead fish,
pancake it dead stick or grease that baby in
the moment before the fuel runs out—
you don't have to set it down on a freeway
or buy a farmer's soy beans after he mows them down,
after you fuel up somehow to fly out again:
you three-point it in, soft as cotton,
as if the wheels start spinning
before you set it down;
bring it in like a spitball
just clearing the powerline at the threshold;
or land in the haze the sun burns into you,
revelation that hurts;
bounce it like an extra point in a football game,
or land in a gift of tongues, multinational
passengers applauding, who step out of the plane
and kneel down like the pope to kiss the earth.
Or do you really want to be Tailspin Tommy smoking in
like hot tuna, full flaps or no flaps,
soft- and short-field landings,
wheel-landings, cross-wind,
touch-and-go, instrument approach?

There is a point
where lift equals weight precisely,
wings talking to air—such a demanding lover,
air is—with a kind of whistle as they crab in

toward the runway, before air lets go
and earth takes over, but easy,
a few skid marks, a slight jolt—easy
as breathing, taking air in, pushing it out again.

3. Manuals

Pitch and yaw, ailerons and rudder,
the old flight manuals illustrated it all;
remember, a caption read, *to relax:*
Some people do it by wiggling their toes.
What good is toe-wiggling when shingling a roof,
or slamming on the brakes, or making love? My wife,
who can cozy her baby toe on top of its neighbor,
said her toes *curl* as we bounce—
not toward a landing,
but to an easier settlement,
releasing each other into the night.

4. Bat in the Movie House

In the house a bat will loop back and forth
in broad lazy-eights, as if suspended
by a long rubber band from the ceiling;

but in the dark other world of the theater,
it flies through the projector's rays
like a German bomber in the blitz—
and my wife, crouching deeply in her seat, says, *Oh God,
    a bat!*
Flying toward the narrow source of the beam,
the bat image grows on the screen like Dracula in 3-D,
above the nervous twitters in the audience,
and the moment ripens: absorbing the projected reds
    and greens,
feeling the audience-warmth with its membrane-wings;
it seems to be flying into us
as, weak-eyed, it nears the ecstasy of light in the lens
until it must peel off, bat shadow
gone from the screen and the bat, in the dark,
invisible again, to find its eventual way
to street lights, and mosquitoes too busy hunting
to sense the radar beam locked onto them, burning.

5. Against Death

When we finished making love,
my wife said she watched me the whole way through—
she was on top, and I wasn't watching in that way,
feeling more like burying my face as usual in her neck
but closed my eyes instead—

not knowing she'd remember me like this
in the camera of her mind, the least exact, most faithful
   record,

so this nature, which was fallen,
is now frozen within her, where she holds me.

Night Aerobatics: Lansing, Michigan, 1942

I barely recognize my father in the photo,
nearly half my age, grim, standing before
the wooden prop. His leather helmet
cuts a widow's peak deep in his forehead;
the winter flightsuit flares out at the rump
like a turnip. It is nearly dusk, and so cold
they hand crank the engines in the hangar
and keep them running while they change students.
The wind chill in those open cockpits is murder;
every day the world slips another notch
into olive drab and gray.
When he takes his students up to three thousand feet
to practice slow-rolls
aiming toward the lit-up capitol dome,
the engine conks out at the inverted end of the roll,
snarls and belches flame out the pipes
once right side up again.
I'd like to tell him
we'll win the war, he'll fly the wounded
back from Karachi and have five sons
who'll move far from home. But he does not know
he is looking into the future,
or that I, once part of him,
look back. And anyway,
he has the present to think about,

to wipe the grease from his goggles
and climb out again through the thick air
in his Howard monoplane and roll slowly,
the engine cutting out and in,
toward that light on the horizon,
until it is all that matters and it is perfect.